The Firefly Detective

J. ROGER DAVIS

ISBN 979-8-88832-605-3 (paperback)
ISBN 979-8-88832-606-0 (digital)

Copyright © 2024 by J. Roger Davis

All rights reserved. No part of this publication may be reproduced, distributed, or transmitted in any form or by any means, including photocopying, recording, or other electronic or mechanical methods without the prior written permission of the publisher. For permission requests, solicit the publisher via the address below.

Christian Faith Publishing
832 Park Avenue
Meadville, PA 16335
www.christianfaithpublishing.com

Printed in the United States of America

I'd like to dedicate this book to my Mom and Dad as
a thank you for encouraging me to follow my dreams
and, most importantly, to follow my heart.

Chapter 1

The farm was an old family farmhouse tucked away in the hills of the Appalachian Mountains where stalks of corn, ready for harvest, stretched towards the sky along the fence at the far end of the property, a place where the sky was clear and it seemed the sun was always shining.

The house was modest with a screened-in front porch. There was a shed in the backyard and an old pickup truck on the side of the house with the license plate missing. A fast-flowing stream separated our farm from our neighbors. Our closest neighbor lived a few miles down a dirt road that twisted and turned past the cemetery and the old Shiloh Baptist Church. If you listened closely, you could hear the preacher's sermon and the congregational singing on Sunday mornings. Most of the folks in these parts attended church, prayed, and worshiped together.

The center of town wasn't much farther down the road. There was a police station, post office, a country store, and a small roadside motel for hikers and travelers who had been detoured due to bad weather or fallen rocks.

My name is James. I remember when I was younger, playing hide and seek and cooling off in the stream with my cousins then running to play kickball and buy penny candy at the country store. Our small town had peach trees, apple trees, and pear trees. Local crops included okra, cucumbers, and tomatoes. Mama would pick vegetables from the garden which she canned, pickled, and preserved for soups and jams for winter and gift-giving.

You could smell the change of seasons in the air. I always noticed when the light shifted. The smell of firewood burning is still my favorite. Freshly mowed grass reminds me of summer, and I loved it when Mama would wash our sheets and hang them on the clothesline to dry. Nothing ever smelled so fresh than those laundered sheets drying in the sun—well, maybe a freshly baked blackberry cobbler resting on the window sill for dessert.

We slept with the windows open. We never locked the front door. At night I could hear every creek in the floorboards and the settling due to cooler temperatures and hear insects buzzing. It seemed night owls, bullfrogs, and crickets were calling to each other. In the evenings, I always loved watching the fireflies flickering about in the field.

I loved hearing Mama's laughter as I settled onto the front porch after dinner. She'd sometimes hum a hymn as she put away leftover dishes from our family meal while my dad sipped on his recent batch of moonshine he kept hidden away. Pap taught him how to make it, he said. He taught him when he was younger so he would grow up in the tradition. Things were different back in those days. Pap made a good business supplying moonshine to the locals and the city folks. They would pay a good penny for it once they learned you had a good recipe. People sure loved Pap. He truly felt that God provided him with all he needed to live a good long life on this earth before he passed. God bless his soul. I miss Pap.

Mama always taught us to say our prayers before going to bed and before eating breakfast, lunch, or dinner. She taught us to pray not just for ourselves but for others in need. I always prayed for all my friends and family, all the animals, and the whole world 'cause there always seemed to be something going on like a tornado or flood, war or fighting somewhere, or people just being mean to each other. I felt safe with my family. I felt safe at the farm.

The story goes there were a lot of unexplained goings-on that happen in these woods. They have never really been explained to me.

Chapter 2

Even as a young boy, I was eager to rise to catch the morning sun. Every morning the smell of breakfast cooking would set the tone for the day. I would spend hours by the stream catching frogs and tadpoles. We would have boat races with bottle caps and search for arrowheads made by earlier native tribes in the layered rock and clay. The way the sunbeams slanted through the trees created a magical shimmer on the ground below. I loved gazing into the light; it was so mesmerizing. The sunbeams felt good on my skin as I stood in its way. Sometimes, I would lie back in the grass and watch the clouds pass on by, forming different shapes and animals I could distinctly identify towering high into a Carolina blue sky.

Sometimes we'd get an afternoon rain. I'd make my way to the house and sit on the front porch and watch the storm clouds roll in over the mountains and hills. Mama soon came running on the porch out of the rain from working in the garden. She was picking collard greens when the storm picked up. Her hands were dirty and soiled. It seems she'd always made a project out of that garden, a sort of meditation for her. After she'd gone inside to clean herself up, she came back out to the porch and sat in her favorite chair.

Apparently, Daddy was in town. Mama said, "I guess it's just me and you holding the fort down this afternoon. Daddy will be back soon."

The rain continued to fall as we both watched the storm from the porch as the wind and rain tossed things about. I could hear the rainwater trickling in rhythm from the rooftop and forming a puddle on the corner of the house. As I gazed into the puddle, I noticed how each raindrop created a ripple effect in the pool of water, pulsating in time to the thunder.

Chapter 3

Suddenly I heard Daddy's car horn coming down the driveway, and Mama had a big smile on her face. I held the door open for him as he made his way into the house with grocery bags. Rainwater dripped all over the floor. "It is nasty out there," he said. Mama replied, "You are soaked!" She was smiling and happy to see him. She kissed him on the cheek. Daddy passed grocery bags to each of us and put produce on the counter and set the remaining bags on the table. He shook the rain off his jacket and kissed Mama on the cheek. Then he sat down at the table to take off his muddy boots.

After washing his hands, he took a bite of my peanut-butter-and-jelly sandwich and patted me on the head. I looked up at him and smiled. Daddy started talking about the weather and how dark skies were rolling into town and how he had been detoured because the bridge was flooded.

I know that I was not supposed to go outside when there's a storm. We were advised not to stray too far into the hills while playing along the stream since it was a part of the Appalachian Trail.

I heard thunder rumble then fade to dead silence. Everything got quiet. I went into the living room and sat on the sofa and covered my ears because I don't like loud noises. I don't like loud noises.

Chapter 4

Later that afternoon, I was watching my favorite show in the living room when I noticed Mama on the phone talking to someone. I overheard her say something was wrong. She didn't know too much about what was going on and was waiting to find out more information. I noticed Daddy was shaking his head.

What is going on? I thought to myself.

She said a little boy has gone missing. They are in town now asking people if they had seen him anywhere.

I watched Daddy search for his keys and wallet.

"I'll go see what I can find out," he said.

"What about your lunch?" Mama asked.

"Wrap it for me," he said. "I'll eat it when I return."

Suddenly he was dashing out the door again, into the pouring rain, down the driveway and mud.

"I'll be back as soon as I can," he said as he drove away.

"If anything were to happen to my babies," Mama said, "I wouldn't know what to do!" She gave me the biggest hug and kiss on the cheek. A special alert flashed across the TV screen. "Turn it up," Mama said. "Turn it up."

Soon after the news, Mama had another phone call. This time about the Shiloh Baptist Church.

Chapter 5

When Mama and I arrived at the church, the sanctuary was loud and filled with townsfolk speculating what may have happened. The police were taking statements and service workers were on standby just in case they found him, and he needed medical attention. Soon, the pastor took the floor and called everyone to order with a prayer: "Dear heavenly Father, we come to you in this time of need. We need you right now…" After the prayer, the missing boy's parents were asked to speak.

"Our boy is missing," his parents said. "If anyone sees him, or if you see anything, please call the police. No detail is too big or too small. Our son is eight years old. He has short cut hair and was wearing a Pittsburgh Steelers T-shirt."

His parents then continued, "When the officer searched our home, there were no signs of foul play. His bedroom window was open. There were fireflies in a jar by his bed."

Our local police chief said, "That's all we have for now. We will begin searching the area. If you are assisting in the search, please sign up with one of our officers before you leave. They will give you a flashlight and a map for tonight's search."

Mama grabbed my hand to keep me close because she could see I was interested in all the activities. I am particularly sensitive to strobe lighting and loud sirens and too much stimulation may cause the onset of a seizure. All the other mothers were gathering their children as well.

When we stepped outside, there was a lot of commotion. I could see Daddy's shadow in flashing blue and red lights. He was helping with the search since he knows the land so well. Daddy knew these woods like the back of his hand. While we were waiting, Mama joined a prayer circle with the other ladies of the church. They were praying for God to intervene.

I thought I was watching a crime scene drama unfold like on the TV show where the detective is on the case, and anyone here could be a suspect. I told Mama I wanted to help with the search. She suggested we let the professionals handle it. It was getting dark and nearing my bedtime.

"There's nothing more we can do until morning," she said.

We said our goodbyes to the other townsfolk, and Mama waved at Daddy, signaling we were leaving.

Dinner was quiet that night. This tragedy and excitement of it all had gotten the best of us. I didn't really eat much because I wasn't hungry.

I grabbed one of the fliers from the church and folded it in my pocket. If I was going to be a detective and help solve this case, I need a special name. My detective name has to be unique. Right then, a firefly flew in through my bedroom window. As I observed him flying about my room, I thought to myself, "The Firefly Detective." What a brilliant idea and it has a nice ring to it. "The Firefly Detective reporting for duty, sir!", that sounds official. I put the firefly in a mason jar then soon let him out to fly around freely in my room with me under the bed covers. I unfolded my flier and turned on my flashlight to get a closer look. *I've seen him before*, I thought to myself.

I understood why Daddy would get so concerned about me. I've wandered off before. I couldn't count the number of nights I've climbed out of my bedroom window to chase fireflies in the corn fields. This was a true mystery.

Maybe aliens beamed him up on their spaceship and took him to some distant planet? What if he fell, or bumped his head, or passed out? Later that night, I heard Daddy pull up into the driveway in his truck. I was hoping there would be an update on the missing boy.

Chapter 6

At sunrise, I was dressed and ready to report for duty. This was the most excitement this town had had in a long while. I heard Mama stirring about in the kitchen. I love the smell of coffee brewing and bacon sizzling in the morning. Daddy emerged from the bedroom rubbing his eyes from a restless night's sleep. "Breakfast is ready if you are hungry," Mama said.

Daddy saw my flashlight and a notepad beside me on the table. "Are you joining the search this morning?" he asked me.

"Yes, sir. I am, sir. Detective Firefly reporting for duty," I replied. Daddy looked to Mama to see if it was alright for me to go.

"Well, he's dressed and ready," Daddy said. They both had a good laugh at my expense.

After breakfast, Daddy and I rode into town to join the search party. There was damage from last night's storm everywhere.

When we approached the group, the police were extending the radius of the search, going deeper into the woods. A few hours later, a police officer blew his whistle. He shouted that he had found a bicycle and noticed that it had a flat tire. This gave the volunteers a lead. The path where the bike was found led to an old abandoned woodshed. As they walked the path, they began to shout out the boy's name, hoping for a response, only to get silence in return.

As they made their way closer to the shed, they found no other clues. All the windows to the shed were broken from tree limbs growing through them. Vines of honeysuckle had twisted and wrapped themselves around the branches. It was obvious no one had been there in years. I could hear the rush of the stream whose levels had risen due to the amount of rain we'd gotten. When I looked inside there was a table, a chair, some bottles, and a wooden chest. In the corner was an old army cot where I found him sleeping. The officer shouted out to the rescue team. They knew it was urgent by the tone of his voice. There was no delay in getting to him, to see if he was hurt.

Chapter 7

Once the EMT arrived, they carried him down the path to the main road where an ambulance was waiting. When they saw his parents, they stopped. His parents were so happy to discover him there of all places. "Thank you, Lord!" his mother cried out and started kissing him on his face. His dad expressed how worried they were. Medical workers examined him for scrapes and bruises and broken bones and gave him some bottled water to prevent dehydration. Once they had him stabilized, they put him in the ambulance, and his parents hopped in to ride to the hospital with him.

As the ambulance drove away, I wondered, *Everyone seemed so surprised when we found him in this place. No one ever talked about it here. It appears he had gotten caught in the rainstorm and had gotten lost while riding his bike. There's nothing but open farms, mountains, and sky between here and there. How did he get all the way down here?* Seems a bit of a mystery to me. The search crew had started to hike back to their cars and trucks parked along the sides of the main road.

After the search crew departed, I noticed the strong aroma of honeysuckle that smelled so sweet in the afternoon breeze. I picked up his bike from the path to put it on the back of my daddy's truck to return to him. "Thank you, Lord," I heard my daddy say. On the way back into the neighborhood, I began to sketch a diagram of the landscape on the flip side of my notebook. The diagram showed we were off-road Highway 24/27, which is the main road through town, and I marked farms and trees and pastures with my colored pencils that lead back to the path near Camp Barnhardt. All the police could gather was the fact that the boy got lost in the storm. The weather report did say there were tornados in the area the other night. I've seen tornadoes hop from mountain top to mountain top. He could have been easily swept away. The winds have been strong enough to level acres of trees, houses, and water towers.

Daddy always said, "If you ever get caught in a tornado, find the nearest shelter, cover your head and pray." That storm could have swept any of us away from here.

A few days passed, and everything had gotten pretty much back to normal, it seemed. I was still thinking about the distance from my house to the woodshed. Looking at a map, following the stream was much quicker than going through town. Later that night, I slipped out of my bedroom window with my flashlight and map. I remember at the shed seeing an old wooden chest and some old photographs and newspaper clippings. I thought maybe there was something in there that would give me some type of clue about that shed. I know I shouldn't be out here. Right then, I noticed a light up ahead in the forest like a series of lights circling the woodshed. It flickered a couple of times as if to signal me to come closer like they do at my bedroom window. I rubbed my eyes as if I was seeing things.

As I drew closer, I began to think, *What if during the storm my friend saw the same lights in the woods and discovered the woodshed the same way I just did?* Maybe there's a connection. Perhaps he followed the light and found safety from the wind and rain. As I got closer to the shed, the clouds gave way to a full moon and suddenly, everything was so clear. I leaned my bike against a nearby tree.

"Hello?" I called into the night.

In a strange way, I didn't feel alone nor was I afraid.

Instead, I heard a voice saying, "Be not afraid. You are safe here."

As I approached the shed entrance, I cleared some broken tree limbs and branches away and pushed through a hinged narrow door. I tapped my flashlight a couple of times to make it stay on and began to look around the tiny dusty room. My batteries were running low. There were old bottles, cans and mason jars, and debris from the roof. I opened the wooden chest to find photographs of a younger woman and a baby. I put the notebook into my satchel for later. Then, I saw a cluster of lighting bugs around the shed. Once again, I began to smell the sweet smell of honeysuckle permeating the air all around me. This is so weird…so strange. Fireflies were flickering in time as if to communicate with me as they danced in the cascading moonlight that reflected off the water downstream. I wanted to stay, but I knew I needed to get back before my parents discovered I was gone.

I jumped on my bike and pedaled home as fast as I could. When I got back to the house, I climbed back through my bedroom window, took off my shoes, and hopped into bed. Lying there I couldn't make sense of what I just experienced. Then, I remembered the notebook. I grabbed my flashlight and opened it. There was a list of Bible verses I could not make out from the faded ink. There were some congregational hymnbooks and sheet music. One of the verses was from Isaiah 41:10: "Fear not, for I am with you; be not dismayed, for I am your God; I will strengthen you, I will help you, I will uphold you with my righteous right hand."

Chapter 8

The next day, word spread through town about my friend. His mom and dad were so relieved and grateful for all the show of support. They were so nice. The doctor said they would like to keep him at the hospital for a few hours before releasing him. It could have been worse. Watching the news, I heard Mama say, "God works in mysterious ways." You could hear the choir singing from the house. The pastor reminded us to never give up on God because today we witnessed a miracle. At that moment, it hit me.

I grabbed my satchel and went to sit on the front porch. Daddy was out with his chain saw cutting up fallen trees like he always does after a big storm, and I watched Mama carry a basket of linen to the clothesline.

She came and sat next to me. I've always liked just sitting with my mama. I said to her, "Mama, I solved the mystery today."

"Yes, you did," she said. So then I told her how "I couldn't figure out how he found that shed the other night. When I discovered his bike, he had a flat tire, so he wasn't riding his bike. He was walking. And I'm sure he went toward the lights."

"What lights?" she asked.

"The fireflies," I replied. "There were hundreds of them. They were all flashing at the same time like a beacon. I saw them for myself. It was so beautiful, Mama. I looked it up online and found out some folks say they are angels. Some say they are our ancestors and spirits of guardians and protectors of the land and the people in the Appalachian Mountains. The fireflies are my friends. They are so beautiful at night."

"Good work, Firefly Detective," Mama said. "I am very proud of you. I see you had an exciting day today with your dad. I love you so much. You are so very special. You are one extraordinary kid…" and on and on she went showering me with compliments on a job well done.

About the Author

J. Roger Davis's upbringings are rooted in the foothills of the Appalachians around campfires, four-part harmonies, and storytelling. His belief in God, his personal life experiences, and his faith in the spirit are the backbones of his appreciation for where he comes from, giving him a voice to speak on the mysticism and spiritualism of the foothills and folklore surrounding the great smoky mountains he writes about.

At an early age, Davis always had a fascination with literature, poetry, and the written word. Davis received his BA in psychology from Pfeiffer University in North Carolina. After college, J. Roger Davis started his career as a presenter and teaching artist, performing poetry and providing poetry performance workshops in classrooms, artist residences in schools, and teacher in-service workshops around the country and abroad, sharing the importance of literacy, reading, reading comprehension, and cognition for people of all ages.

www.ingramcontent.com/pod-product-compliance
Lightning Source LLC
Chambersburg PA
CBHW040119150726
48005CB00013B/1793